My first 500 words

Illustrated By Jazer Cerojano-Basan

We are Julie and Jacob, brother and sister, and together, we will take you on a journey through our lives. From our messy bedroom, to our school classroom, we want to show you some of the words we come across in our daily lives! Around the border of every illustration, there will be 25 objects with words for you to find in the illustration!

Happy searching!

Dear parents: Thank you for making the purchase, we really hope you enjoy this book. If you have the chance, then all feedback is greatly appreciated. For best use: get the child to locate each object within the illustration. In each illustration, there are objects that are listed in the other illustrations throughout this book, so ask your child about those objects for more of a challenge. Once finished, go over this book several more times and watch your child's understanding of vocabulary progress!

WANDERLUST PRESS

No part of this book may be copied, reproduced or sold without express permission from the owner.

Copyright Wanderlust Press 2021. All rights reserved.

OUR BODY

Smile
Head

Nose

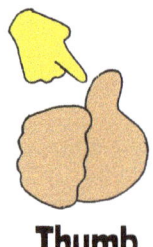
Thumb

Hair

Teeth

Mouth

Lips

Eyebrow

Tongue

Ears

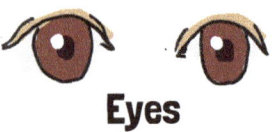
Eyes

FAMILY

 **Earrings**
 **Handbag**
 **Necklace**
 **Happy**
 **Angry**

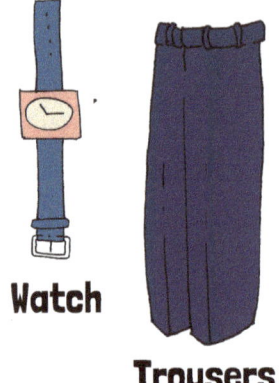 **Watch** **Trousers**

 **Skirt**

 **T Shirt**

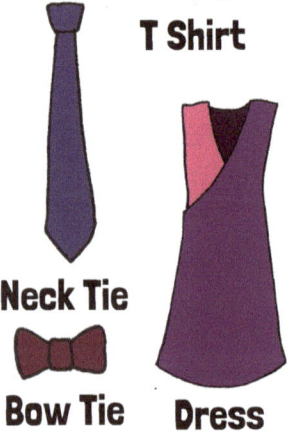 **Neck Tie** **Bow Tie** **Dress**

 **Suit**

BEDROOM

 Pillow
 Books
 Piggy Bank

 Curtains

Flute

 Drums

 Planet   Stars

 Cupboard

 Lamp   Pyjamas

 Toy Box

BATHROOM

 **Deodorant**

 **Duck**

 **Mirror**

Hairbrush

Perfume

Comb   **Toothpaste**

Hot   **Cold**

Tap

Towel

Clean

Dirty

DINING ROOM

Bowl

Glass

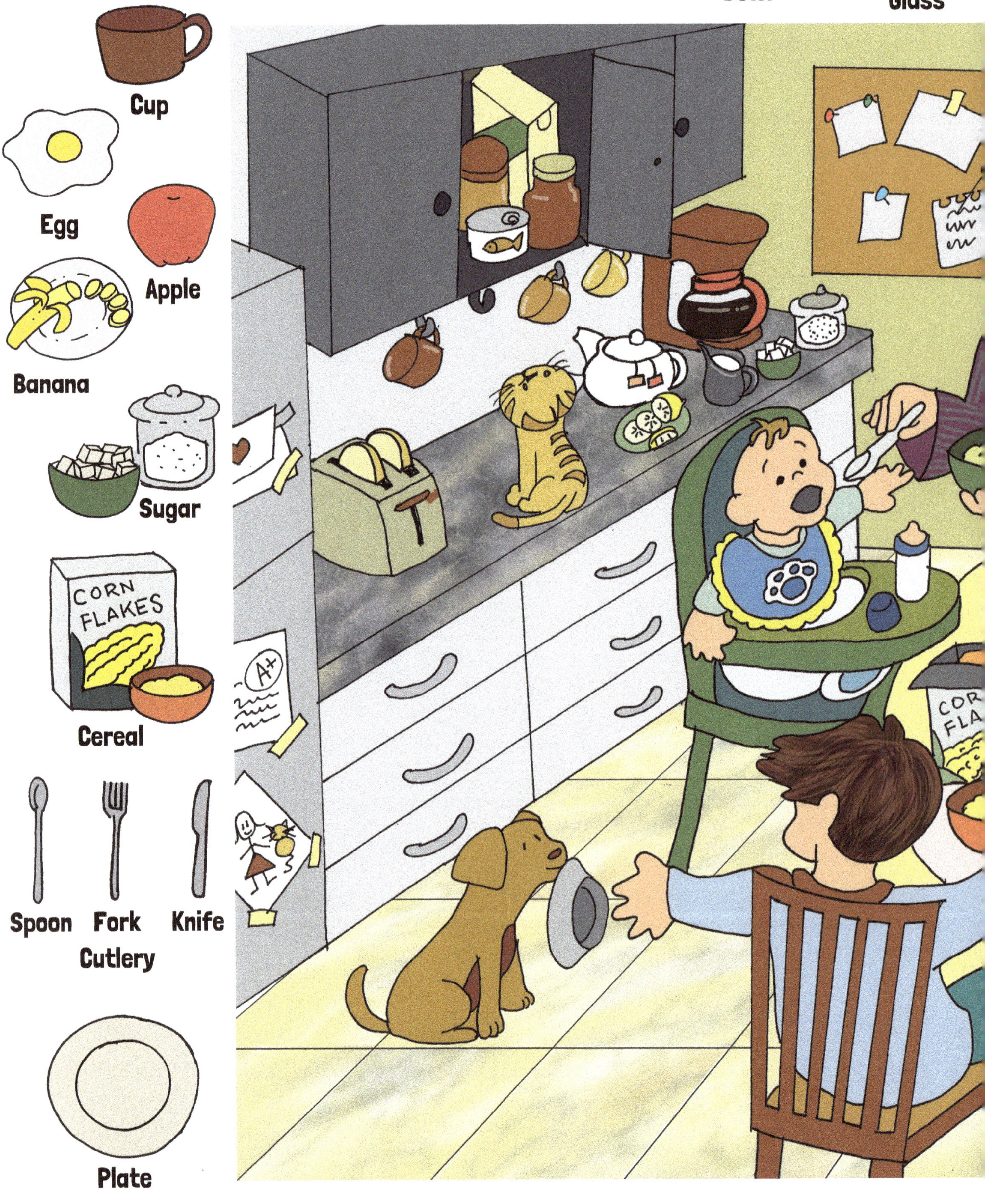

Cup

Egg

Apple

Banana

Sugar

Cereal

Spoon Fork Knife
Cutlery

Plate

Microwave **Pot** **Pan** **Kettle** **Ladle** **Spatula** **Dishwasher** **Oven** **Stove** **Apron** **Freezer** **Refrigerator**

LIVING ROOM

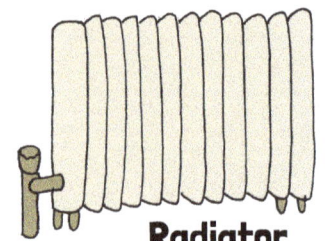
Radiator

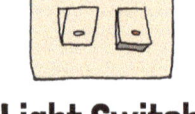
Light Switch

Armchair

Couch

Slippers

Plant

Telephone   Cable

Magazines

Picture

Lamp

Carpet

PORCH

Ironing Board

Letterbox

Boots

Letter

Shoes

Closet

Cat Flap

Bag

Keyhole

Coat Hanger

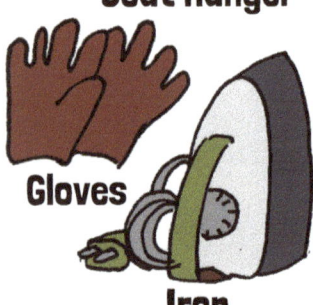
Gloves

Iron

GARAGE

 Paint
 Paintbrush Toolbox
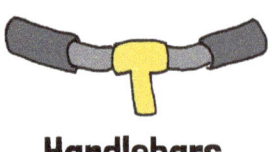 Handlebars

 Nails
 Hammer

 Steering Wheel

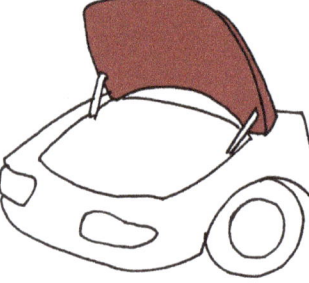 Hood

 Oil Can

Dustpan

 Scissors

 Bicycle

GARDEN

 Hedge

 Birdhouse

 Compost

 Branch

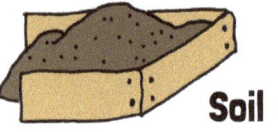 Soil

Fence

 Flower

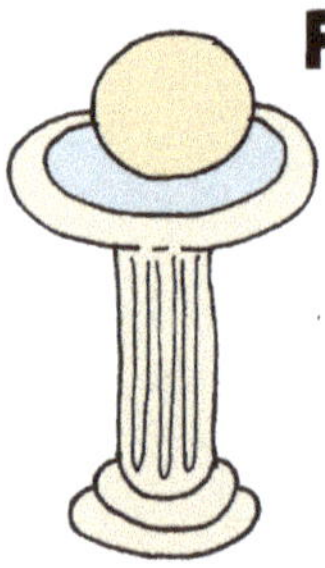

Birdbath

 Shed

Gnome

 Lawnmower

 Greenhouse

CLASSROOM

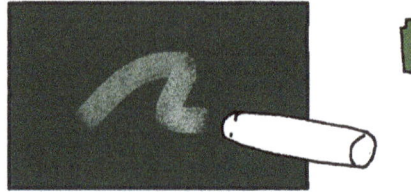
Chalk

Lego

Dictionary

Lunchbox

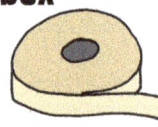
Tape

Eraser

Drawing   Globe

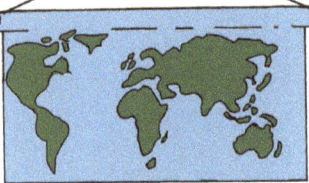
World Map

Numbers

Blackboard

CARNIVAL AT THE PARK

NEIGHBORHOOD

Crossing

Ice Cream Van

Ambulance

Car

Drain

Scooter

Postbox

Road

Traffic Light

Motorcycle

Skateboard

Mailbox

Parcel

TOWN CENTRE

Shops

Airplane

Fountain

Park

Bank

Airport

Flag Theatre

Statue Church

Library

FARM

 Chicken
 Turkey
 Logs Axe
 Wheat

 Farmer Pitchfork

 Pig

 Cow Udder

 Calf Rabbit

 Pen

 Combine Harvester

COUNTRYSIDE

Town

Sun

Waterfall

Dam

Mountain

Lorry

Factory

Hot Air Balloon

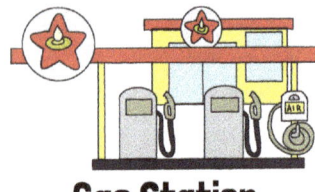
Gas Station

Tunnel

BEACH

Boat

Surfboard

Shark

Dolphin

Lifeguard

Turtle

Shells

Cliff

Crab

Lighthouse

CONGRATULATIONS

...FOR COMPLETING THIS BOOK!

WOULD YOU LIKE AN EXTRA CHALLENGE?
SEE BELOW.

CAN YOU LOCATE THESE EXTRA ITEMS IN THIS BOOK?

Spaghetti

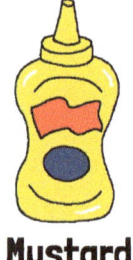
Mustard

Hen

Windmill

Laptop

Suncream

Moped

Robot

Lobster

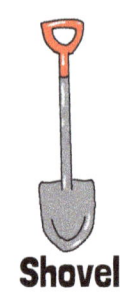
Shovel

Oil

Bib

www.ingramcontent.com/pod-product-compliance
Lightning Source LLC
Chambersburg PA
CBHW041228240426
43661CB00013B/1173